Drawing Is Awesome!

DRAWING AWESOME
CARS

Damien Toll

WINDMILL
BOOKS ™

Contents

Introduction

Drawing is a fun and rewarding hobby for both children and adults alike. This book is designed to show how easy it is to draw great pictures by building them in simple stages.

What you will need

Only basic materials are required for effective drawing. These are:

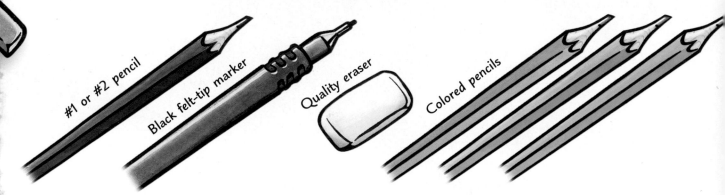

#1 or #2 pencil

Black felt-tip marker

Quality eraser

Colored pencils

These will be enough to get started. Avoid buying the cheapest pencils. Their leads often break off in the sharpener, even before they can be used. The leads are also generally too hard, making them difficult to see on the page.

Cheap erasers also cause problems by smudging rather than erasing. This often leaves a permanent stain on the paper. By spending a little more on art supplies in these areas, problems such as these can be avoided.

When purchasing a black marker, choose one to suit the size of your drawings. If you draw on a large scale, a thick felt-tip marker may be necessary. If you draw on a medium scale, a medium-point marker will do and if on a small scale, a 0.3 mm, 0.5 mm, 0.7 mm, or 0.8 mm felt-tip marker will work best.

The Stages

Simply follow the lines drawn in orange on each stage using your #1 or #2 pencil. The blue lines on each stage show what has already been drawn in the previous stages.

1.

2.

3.

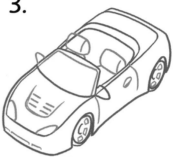

In the final stage the drawing has been outlined in black and the simple shape and wire-frame lines erased. The shapes are only there to help us build the picture. We finish the picture by drawing over the parts we need to make it look like our subject with the black marker, and then erasing all the simple shape lines.

4.

Included here is a sketch of a sports car as it would be originally drawn by an artist.

These are how all the cars in this book were originally worked out and drawn. The orange and blue stages you see above are just a simplified version of this process. The drawing here has been made by many quick pencil strokes working over each other to make the line curve smoothly. It does not matter how messy it is as long as the artist knows the general direction of the line to follow with the black marker at the end. The pencil lines are erased and a clean outline is left. Therefore, do not be afraid to make a little mess with your #1 or #2 pencil, as long as you do not press so hard that you cannot erase it afterwards.

5.

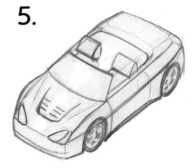

Grids made of squares are set behind each stage in this book. Make sure to draw a grid lightly on your page so it does not press into the paper and show up after being erased. Artist tips have also been added to show you some simple things that can make your drawing look great. Have fun!

Truck

With their loud deep horns, huge wheels, and big engines, trucks are the biggest vehicles on our roads. They range in size from the lighter delivery trucks to the 18-wheel semi-trailers. Most trucks have a horn that you pull down, rather than press with your finger. Their main use is to transport goods. The largest truck in the world can carry around 440 tons!

1.

Begin by drawing a grid with three equal squares going across and down.

Start by drawing the squarish shapes in the correct position on the grid.

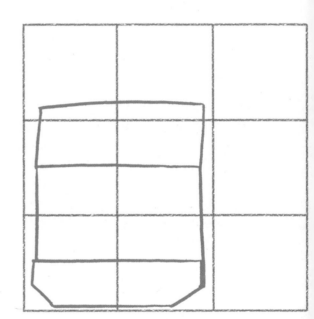

2.

Draw the truck's grill and light panels. Draw in the two windshield windows. Define the cabin and add the side window.

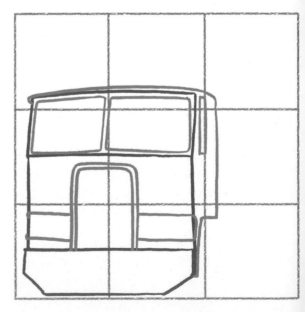

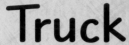

3.

Draw the lines for the grill. Add the headlights and place for the license plate. Draw in the exhaust pipes, horns, lights, and the windbreak on the roof.

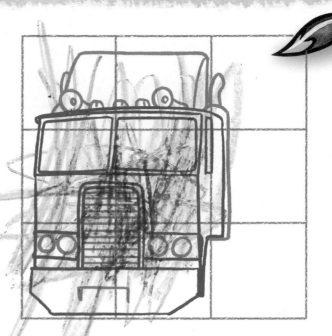

4.

Finish by drawing the trailer. Make sure your truck's wheels are tall and skinny.

5.

Outline your drawing and erase the pencil lines. Color your drawing. The graphics on trucks have lots of different patterns. Maybe you could invent some of your own for the front and side of your truck.

Supercar

Supercars are the cars people dream about owning. A lot of time is put into designing them so that they look really good and have powerful engines. They have an aerodynamic body so they can cut through the air, like an airplane. Supercars are very fast and very, very expensive.

1.

Begin by drawing a grid with four equal squares going across and two down.

Draw in the long, curved shape highest on the grid. Draw in the bottom curve, taking notice of the kinks at the corners of the triangle. Put in the lines to make the two triangles.

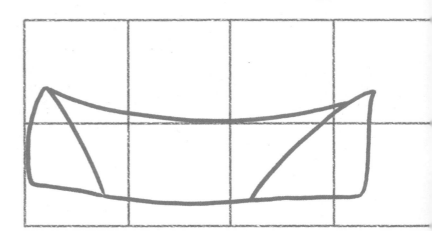

2.

Draw in the angled lights and air intake at the front of the car. Draw the parts of the front tires that are visible. Draw in the wheels at the side and the line between them.

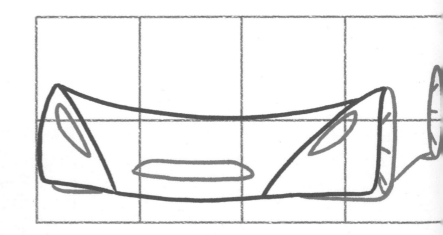

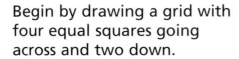

3.

Draw in the small air intakes in the front triangles. Add in the rounded shape for the windshield. Draw in the line for the side and add the side air intake.

4.

Draw on the wing at the rear of the car to finish.

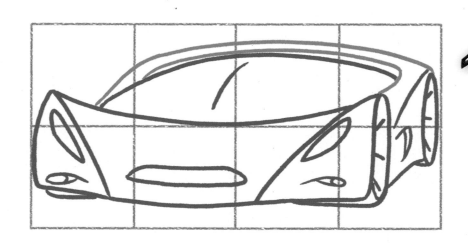

5.

Outline your supercar and erase the pencil lines. Color your drawing. Red is often associated with speed and works well on this supercar.

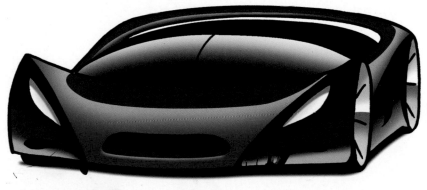

Sports Car

Sports cars are low, designed for quick response and good handling. They generally have two doors, two seats, and a roof that can be taken off. Sport cars are made for luxury, with all the latest car gizmos and gadgets. A sports car is really fun to drive on a nice sunny day.

1.

Begin by drawing a grid with four equal squares going across and three down.

Then draw the side of the car and a little of the front.

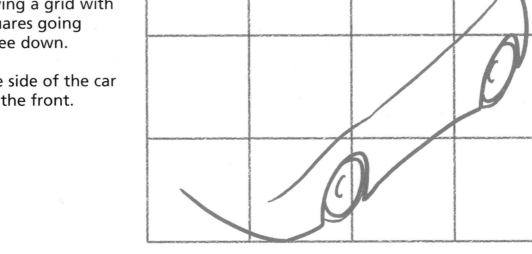

2.

Continue to draw the rest of the body and windshield. Add the side mirror.

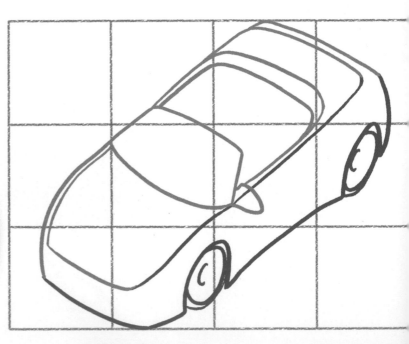

3.

Add the lights and front grill. Define the windshield and hood details. Add the far side mirror and seats. Draw in the door lines and handles. Finish by adding sporty shapes for the wheels.

Artist Tip:

Light is reflected best on corners. Here we have added little light spots on some of the corners of the car to help it look shiny. To add these highlights, color your whole car first and then look for little corners to highlight with a white dot. You can use white paint or even a correction pen for this. Little details like light-spot reflections can greatly enhance our drawings.

4.

Sports cars come in many different colors. This one is green, but you could make it any color you like.

Rally Car

Rally cars are off-road racers, driving at incredible speeds through mud, snow, and gravel. The navigator sits next to the driver, giving instructions on how to take the next turn. A lot of time is spent sideways and making split-second decisions about where to steer the car. Rally drivers have great reflexes.

1.

Begin by drawing a grid with four equal squares going across and three down.

Now, draw in the bumper bar and lights. Add the tight arch where the wheel will be.

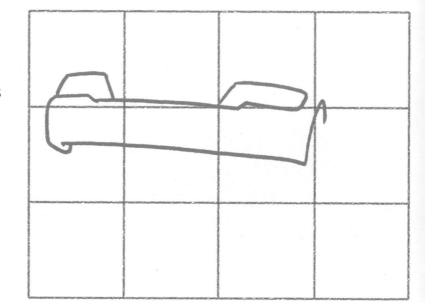

2.

Draw on the details on the bumper bar and grill. Add a curved line for the hood and the windshield above.

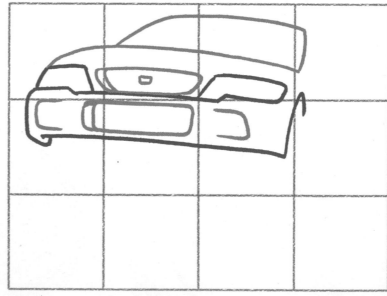

3.

Draw the fog lights on the bumper. Draw the front wheel and body side.

4.

Draw the roof line to the side window. Add lines for the doors and the door handles. Draw the top of the drivers' helmets. Add on the hood lines. Draw the shape for the rear wing. Draw in the bottom of the car and the rough ground below.

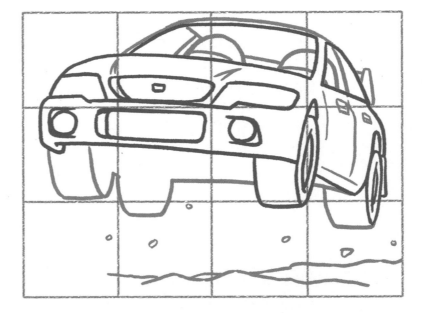

5.

Here we have made up a color scheme and number for the rally car. You could make up your own pattern and put your favorite number on it.

Motorcycle

There are a few different types of motorcycles, such as off-road and touring motorcycles. Not all of them have two wheels – some types come with three or four. Motorcycles are very zippy compared to cars. They don't use much fuel and are very easy to park, which makes them great for transport. Motorbikes are lots of fun!

1.

Begin by drawing a grid with four equal squares going across and three down.

First draw the body shape, being careful to construct the lines in their correct place on the grid. Add in the exhaust pipe.

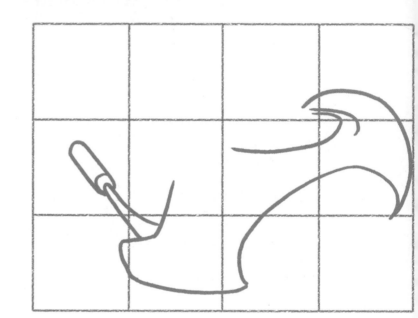

2.

Draw the leg first, followed by the arm and hand. Draw the line for the top of the gas tank. Draw on the cross-arm under the leg shape. Draw the piece of fork under the body.

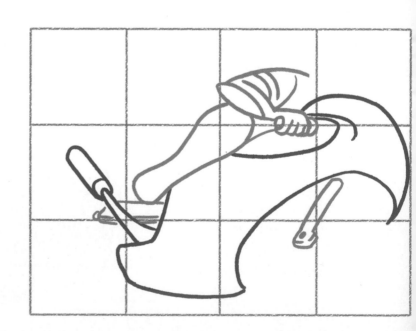

3.

Define the knee pad and boot with some curved lines on the leg. Draw in the rear and front wheels and details.

4.

Draw the helmet. Next, draw a line through the top of the body for the visor. Draw in the wheel cover on the front wheel. Add the rear and the seat of the bike. Finish by putting in the drive chain near the back wheel.

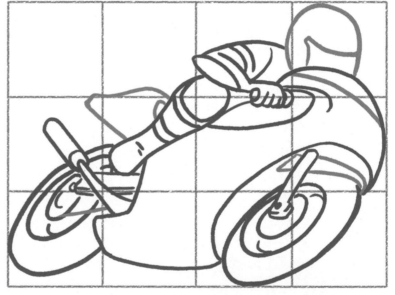

5.

Here we have designed a simple pattern and a made-up sponsor for our racing bike. See if you can come up with a pattern and sponsor for your bike.

Model T

In the early 1900s, cars were just toys for really rich people. Henry Ford thought it would be a good idea if almost everyone could afford a car. So in 1908 he released the Model T, a car that was affordable for the average American. Henry Ford sold a lot of his cars and by 1914, he had made more cars than any other company.

1.

Begin by drawing a grid with four equal squares going across and three down.

Start with the roof and windows. Notice the curved line for the beginning of the hood.

2.

Draw in the hood lines and the light. Add the grill. Finish this stage with the wheel covers.

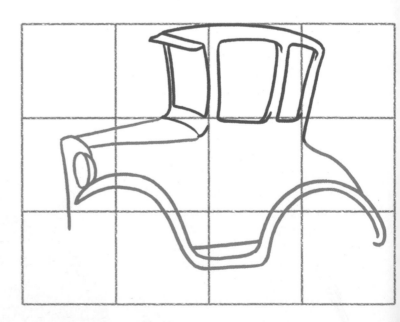

3.

Draw in the wheels. Add the far headlight, grill line, and wheel cover. Draw in the spare tire on the rear and the door handle.

4.

Draw in the door lines and the spokes for the wheels.

5.

Here we have colored the Model T black. This was a common color for the early car. If we had colored it completely black, however, it would look like a black blob. By adding some white light reflections the car still looks black, but the different parts can be seen.

Land Speed Car

Land speed cars are the fastest cars in the world. They often look a lot like an airplane because of their streamlined designs, which lets them cut through the air really quickly. Land speed cars can even have one or two jet engines to power their wheels. The record for the fastest land speed car is 763.035 mph (1,237.985 km/h)! That's faster than the speed of sound!

1.

Begin by drawing a grid with four equal squares going across and three down.

Then draw the leaf shape for the cabin. Study the body shape to draw it accurately.

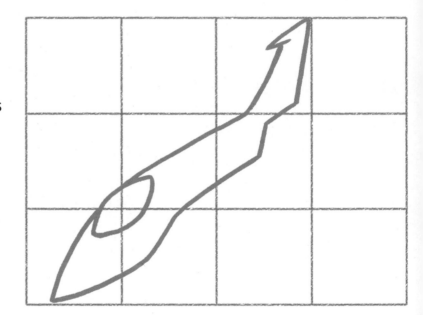

2.

Draw in the jet turbines on either side of the body shape. Notice how only a small amount of the far turbine can be seen. Draw in a small part of the rear wheel cover on this side.

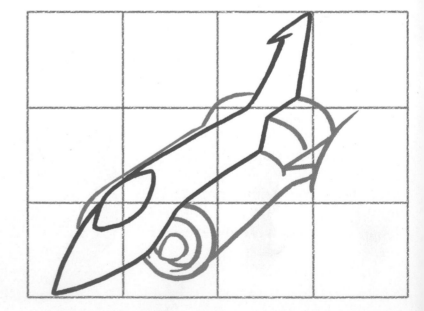

3.

Finish with the wheel covers.

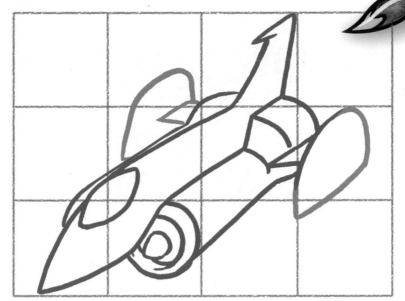

Artist Tip:

Things look smooth and shiny when a reflection is added. This is how it works:

1. This dotted line along the side represents a reflection off the ground. It could be reflecting a straight flat plane. If we were to reflect mountains, the reflection line would go up and down.

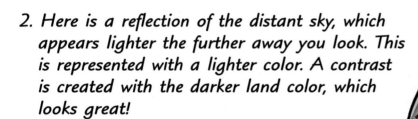

2. Here is a reflection of the distant sky, which appears lighter the further away you look. This is represented with a lighter color. A contrast is created with the darker land color, which looks great!

3. The lighter color rises into a deeper blue, which represents the color overhead. This same contrast reflection principle can be seen on many of the cars in this book. Try it, it really works!

4. The reflection of the flames can be seen on the back of the car, making it look more real.

4.

Outline your drawing and erase the pencil lines. Land speed cars do not have any specific color so you could make it any color you like. Happy coloring!

Family Car

Family cars are made for safely carrying a family and their luggage from location to location. They are used to transport kids to school and bring the groceries home. These cars aren't built for speed, but a lot of time still goes into designing them to make them as safe as possible. Family cars are usually large and spacious.

1.

Begin by drawing a grid with three equal squares going across and down.

Draw the lights and bumper bar in the correct position on the grid. Keep the line going smoothly from the bottom of the bumper, around the wheel arch, and along the body. Continue that line through the rear wheel arch, bumper, and tailgate.

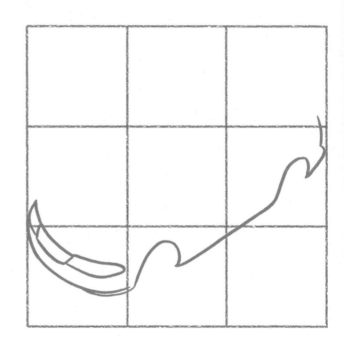

2.

Draw in the hood line going up over the windshield, roof and around to the tailgate. Add the windshield. Draw the side window, keeping it at the same angle as the line for the bottom of the car.

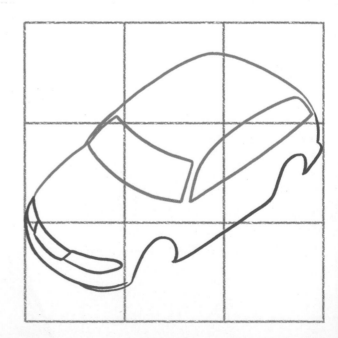

3.

Add the side mirrors. Draw a line from the windshield to the bumper. This will define the light and indicator. Add the side of the bumper and the lines on the hood and roof. Draw in the wheels to complete this stage.

4.

Add the dividing lines on the windows, doors, and bumper. Finish with the door handles and the rear light.

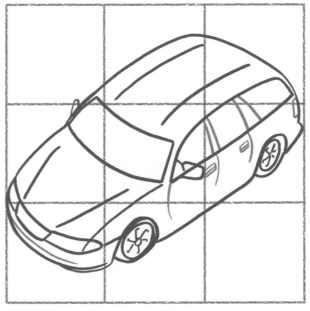

5.

Outline your drawing and erase the pencil lines. Family cars come in many different colors, so you could color your car any color you like.

Dune Buggy

Dune buggies are a cross between a car and a go-cart. They are made for fun! Dune buggies fly up and down sand dunes, and race along dirt roads. They have large tires that can go on all types of surfaces: tar, gravel, dirt, sand, and even snow! A lot of people like to race their dune buggies. Another name for a dune buggy is a "sandrail."

1.

Begin by drawing a grid with three equal squares going across and down.

Next, draw the wheels. Notice they are on slightly different angles to each other.

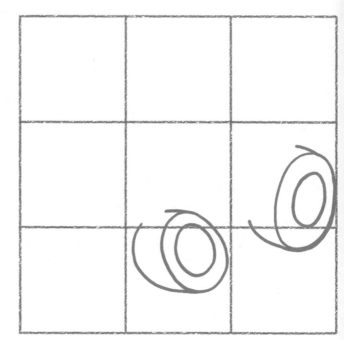

2.

Add the inside details of the wheels. Draw in the side of the body. Add the lights and finish this stage with the bumper bar.

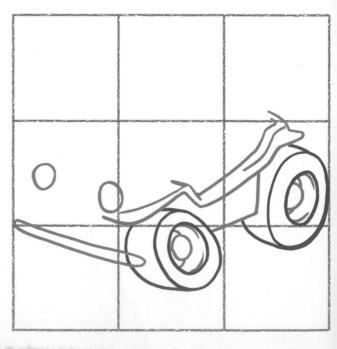

3.

Draw in the roll-bar at the rear. Add the side line, hood and windshield. Draw in the light cases.

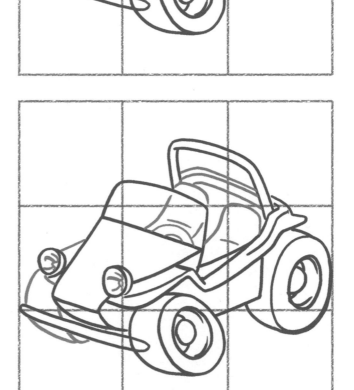

4.

Add the rear of the buggy between the roll-bars. Draw in the steering wheel and the seats. Add the lines on the inside of the lights. Draw the wheel cover on the far side and the wheel under it to finish.

5.

Outline your drawing and erase the pencil lines. Since this is a fun car, we have used bright colors to make it more lively. You could draw someone driving it really fast across the sand.

Bumper Car

Banging into your friends or unsuspecting strangers, then racing away to escape someone else crashing into you, that's the bumper car experience! They are an attraction at most fairs, shows and amusement parks. The cars are normally powered by electricity and most of the time they don't go as fast as you want them to. Bumper cars quite often turn calm and safe drivers into crash-seeking hooligans!

1.

Begin by drawing a grid with four equal squares going across and three down.

Then start with drawing the eyes and brow in the correct position on the grid. Add the nose, mouth, and the line for the shoulder.

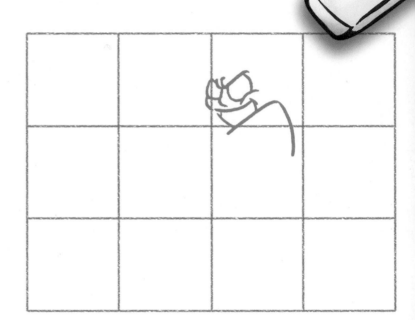

2.

Add the hair and arms with the hands at the end. Draw the steering wheel and then the surrounding lines for the car.

3.

Draw in the chin on the boy. Draw in the rest of the car.

4.

Draw the eyes and the mouth on the car. Add the boy's eyes. Finish with the rubber surround on the bottom of the car.

5.

Outline your drawing and erase the pencil lines. Color your bumper car in your favorite colors.

Custom Car

A lot of time and money is spent on these cars to make them look, sound, feel, and run at peak performance. These cars are entered in shows and various competitions against other custom cars. Shiny paint jobs, big mag wheels, and engines that poke out of the hood are typical features of a custom car. This type of car is made for its "wow" factor.

1.

Begin by drawing a grid with four equal squares going across and three down.

Now start drawing in the bumper bar. Add the indicator lights and the arc for the grill area. Draw in the wheel arch and front wheel. Draw in the rest of the body and the rear wheel.

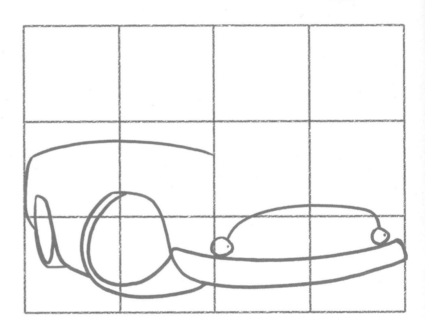

2.

Draw in the lights' circles. Draw the pieces for the grill and inside areas. Add the body shape above the grill and the engine parts. Add the detail on the inside of the wheels.

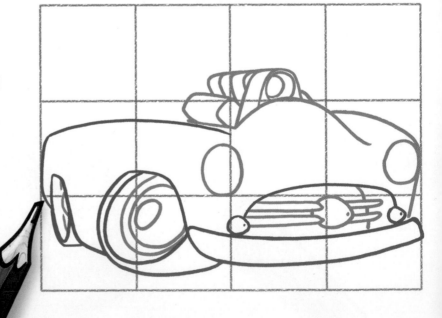

3.

Draw in the rest of the engine parts. Add the reflection lines in the lights and the circle in the grill. Draw the roof and windows. Finish with some short lines for the doors and get ready to outline.

Artist Tip:

There are a few secrets to drawing great cartoony cars. They are:

1. *When drawing the side, have the distance between the wheels as close as possible, while still maintaining the normal wheel size.*

2. *Make the body really tall.*

3. *Make the side windows and roof line really short.*

These simple but effective principles will have you cartooning great cars in no time!

4.

Color your car. Study the metal parts closely. A light blue color on top that fades into white, a black line through the middle, and a dark gray that fades make it look shiny.

4x4

Real 4x4s are off-road cars. Jacked up high with added suspension and monster wheels, they force their way over huge obstacles and up really steep hills. "Four-wheel drive" means that if two wheels are bogged in mud, the other two can pull the car free. A stop at the car wash is often needed after the 4x4 has been through the mud all day.

1.

Begin by drawing a grid with three equal squares going across and down.

Next, draw the wheels. Notice how they are on different angles to each other. Draw in the rocky ground. Check to make sure you have placed everything correctly on your grid.

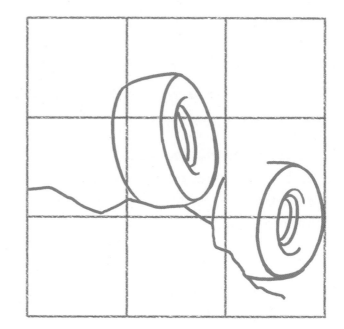

2.

Draw in the other front wheel. Draw the bumper bar and wheel arches. Add the line across the bottom of the truck and the rear wheel arch.

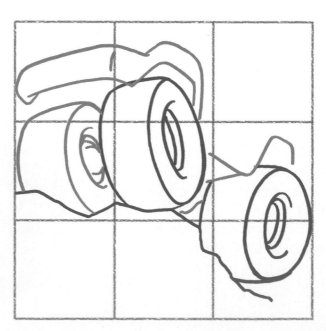

3.

Draw in the hood and cabin structure. Add the side window shape and the bottom door line going into the rear wheel arch cover.

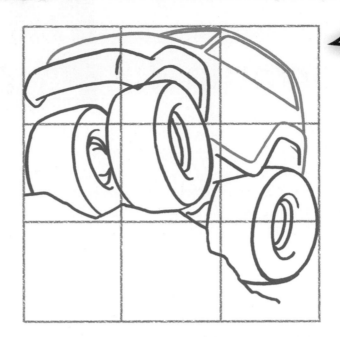

4.

Draw in the grill and lights. Add the license plate area. Divide the side window into individual windows and add door lines. Finish with the door handles.

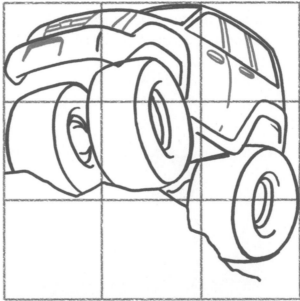

5.

Outline your drawing and erase the pencil lines. You could draw some more of the rocky road here or even put the car on top of a really high mountain.

Formula 1

A Formula 1 car is very expensive.
Lots of time is spent designing and maintaining these cars to make them as fast as possible. Millions of dollars are spent before a Formula 1 team wins an event. Formula 1 drivers have to know their car really well so they can speed around the track as fast as possible. A Formula 1 car can go over 200 mph (320 km/h)!

1.

Begin by drawing a grid with three equal squares going across and down.

Draw a rounded "V" for the nose cone. Add the wings on either side.

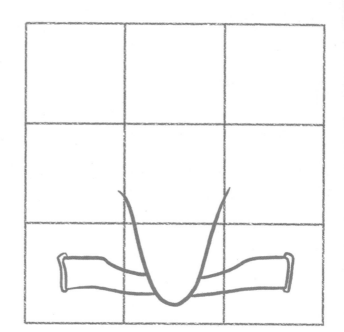

2.

Draw the wheels on either side and parts of the air intakes beside them. Add the curved shape for the cabin opening.

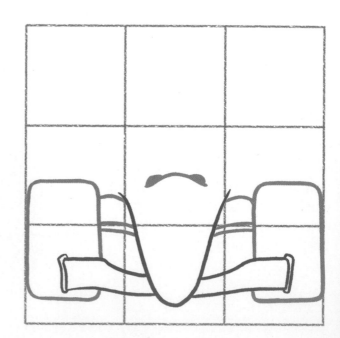

3.

Draw in the helmet and central air intake above the driver's head. Add the mirrors on either side. Draw the body shape to finish this stage.

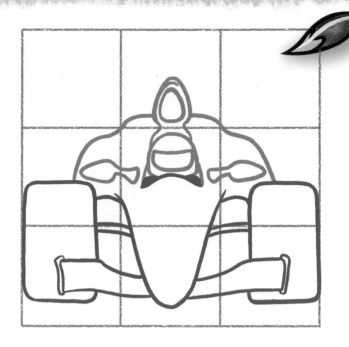

4.

Draw in the rear wing and wheel wings. Add the back wheels. Draw in the steering rod lines to the front wheels to finish.

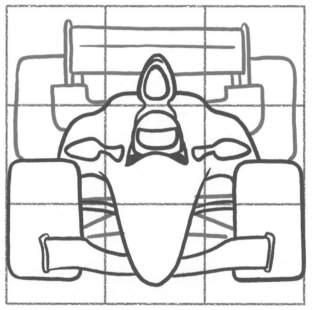

5.

Here we have colored the car with a simple color scheme of orange and white. You could invent your own color scheme and even your own team design, and also put it on the truck, rally car, and motorcycle pictures in this book.

Van

Vans make good family cars because they have room for all the people and their gear. Most vans have the engine underneath the driver and front passenger. Sometimes if people want to carry something really big, they fold down the back seats so they can fit the large object in.

1.

Begin by drawing a grid with four equal squares going across and three down.

Start by drawing the entire outside shape of the van. Be careful to note where each line intersects the grid lines.

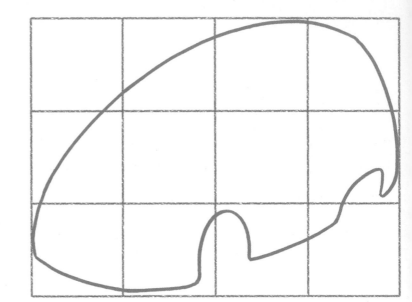

2.

Draw in the curved rectangle side door. Add the round shape for the windshield which comes to a point at the front. Draw in the dashboard and small air intakes at the bottom of the car's front.

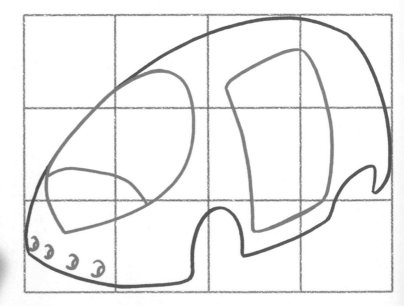

3.

Draw in the wheels and side mirrors. Add lines to define the front lights. Draw in the steering wheel.

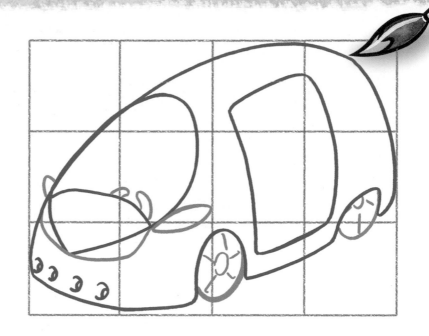

4.

Draw the two curving lines for the side window. The top one continues on over the windshield. Add the seats to finish.

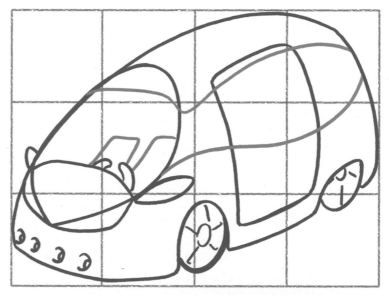

5.

Outline your drawing, erase the pencil lines and color. See if you can make up a futuristic town the van could be driving through.

Published in 2015 by **Windmill Books,**
an Imprint of Rosen Publishing,
29 East 21st Street, New York, NY 10010.

Copyright © 2015 by Hinkler Books

Written and illustrated by Damien Toll.
With thanks to Jared Gow.

Library of Congress Cataloging-in-Publication Data
Toll, Damien.
 Drawing awesome cars / Damien Toll.
    pages cm. — (Drawing is awesome!)
 Includes index.
ISBN 978-1-4777-5460-3 (pbk.)
ISBN 978-1-4777-5478-8 (6 pack)
ISBN 978-1-4777-5471-9 (library binding)
1. Automobiles in art—Juvenile literature.
2. Drawing—Technique—Juvenile literature.
 I. Title.
 NC825.A8T65 2015
 743'.89629222—dc23
                                    2014027092

Manufactured in the United States of America
CPSIA Compliance Information: Batch # CW15WM: For Further Information contact
Rosen Publishing, New York, New York at 1-800-237-9932